CHELATE

CHELATE JAY BESEMER

BROOKLYN ARTS PRESS | NEW YORK

CHELATE
© 2016 JAY BESEMER

ISBN-13: 978-1-936767-49-6

Cover photograph by Seung-Hwan Oh (*Impermanence_DavidHyun*, 2013, from his 'Impermanence' series).
Cover and interior design by Martin Rock.
Edited by Joe Pan.

All rights reserved. No part of this publication may be reproduced by any means existing or to be developed in the future without written consent by the publisher.

Published in the United States of America by:
Brooklyn Arts Press
154 N 9th St #1
Brooklyn, NY 11249
WWW.BROOKLYNARTSPRESS.COM
INFO@BROOKLYNARTSPRESS.COM

Distributed to the trade by Small Press Distribution / SPD
www.spdbooks.org

Library of Congress Cataloging-in-Publication Data

Names: Besemer, Jay, author.
Title: Chelate : poems / by Jay Besemer.
Description: First edition. | Brooklyn, NY : Brooklyn Arts Press, [2016] | "Distributed to the trade by Small Press Distribution / SPD"--T.p. verso.
Identifiers: LCCN 2016010211 | ISBN 9781936767496 (pbk. : alk. paper)
Classification: LCC PS3602.E775 A6 2016 | DDC 811/.6--dc23
LC record available at https://lccn.loc.gov/2016010211

First Edition, Second Printing

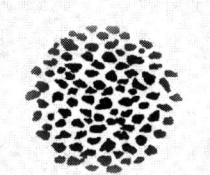

CONTENTS

XENOPHILIA

[time for a dream language] 15
[welcome to your immaculate dream universe] 16
[we're speaking in code] 17
[when the structure cracks open] 18
[the origami contrivances are burning] 19
[activate a mouth for every encounter] 20
[the nothingness that gleams in the night] 21
[everyone speaks at once] 22
[this wind has a heart that stretches] 23
[who wants to play with my rainy day] 24
[umbilical wilderness intrudes] 25
[hear the tent music from the hillside] 26
[we beat into the dusk] 27
[drink this twilight before it fades] 28
[the thousand galaxies commune in our hearts] 29
[expletive deleted] 30
[trypophobic ancestors render me addlepated] 31
[fall asleep & a small sound escapes] 32
[our inclement source material] 33
[prowling pink for saxifrage] 34
[interpretation of cloud patterns] 35
[destined to the bunker] 36

MAKING & UNMAKING
[training day dawns over my depleted town] 39
[nobody can be one thing all the time] 40
[a fragment of certainty breaks off] 41
[the trend of the ivy along these walls] 42
[mollusk mentation in my momentary lapse] 43
[exhaustion of the warmth of motivation] 44
[the air & the hand work in each other's territories] 45
[that bulky vocoder in your bin] 46
[friends, there are some books you will not want to read] 47
[our adaptive strategy takes it out of the park] 48
[static, frost] 49
[i'm cooling these crimes] 50
[sometimes a symbol stalks up behind] 51
[ordinary merrymakers disturb the mahout] 52
[my philosophers are all in love with one another] 53

ADJUSTMENT DISORDER
[the interior has debatable contours] 57
[too much talk] 58
[aspergillus] 59
[just think of that song you heard] 60
[ears to the ground] 61
[exist in a state of unknowing] 62
[nothing comes easily] 63

[the flayed man & his heartthrob] 64
[the older i get the more things tend to blur into each other] 65
[prepaid disaster, its lip on fire] 66
[under the pardonable bridge of fear] 67
[tornado school] 68
[seven of us started] 69
[the dead lands open & the night turns on its shadow] 70
[all these catacombs & flames] 71
[codes] 72
[asphalt word] 73
[how to edit a life] 74
[what we wait for remains unreachable] 75
[how many ways to say that the body is light] 76
[i like the diamond that sprouts in the spaces between words] 77
[& these stars awake in your belly] 78
[do not sing too loudly of the mastery of desire] 79
[i am without wings] 80
[don't call us] 81
[that grim drum beats in sleep] 82
[the body between sleep & waking] 83
[they say it's best to take it in stages] 84

MY INHERITANCE
[i'm not interested in bombs or babies] 87
[what's my name] 88

[sorry doesn't hold a world] 89
[the rack of cymbals in my body] 90
[someone waits to be let in] 91
[the dragon looks tired] 92
[the forest will find you] 93
[life is about to change] 94
[this dark projection can be a burden] 95
[tendons tell stories] 96
[erasing one file] 97
[i scare the neighbors] 98
[i want nothing but my] 99
[during the day the signals shift & fade] 100
[my questions multiply] 101
[i am talking & the sand is listening] 102
[separate your hazards] 103
[this sound is distracting me] 104

ORDINARY WEAR & TEAR
[& what has it given me] 107
[distance & dishes accumulate rapidly] 108
[it's time] 109
[the marshals are circling again] 110
[not exalted in the way you mean] 111
[the cities of the body are populated by question & answer] 112
[the man with dead words hanging from his body] 113

[this wish i have for your blessing] 114
[every morning there is the male milk-bath] 115
[sky-hopping] 116
[there is a certain nudity in this experience] 117
[the judge sits in a bucket & i think that's OK] 118
[who will share my pornography of meaning] 119
[if it isn't clear by now, then it's muddy] 120
[now is a time for speaking secrets in secret ways] 121

XENOPHILIA

time for a dream language : take tales of galactic standard : need for filenames : i have fear : i am fear : the nuances of being or experience : shoot me out to the stars : your great pod an invitation : i count on no particular reception : my destination is all around me : work & know : sow in mist-covered ground : what has come before is still ahead : understand how impossible the goal of meeting others' expectations : to speak in their language : this life so far from home ::

welcome to your immaculate dream universe : the sterile dirt of pleasure : the programmable bird on a cartwheel : we go round & round : you want a schedule of events : there are no terraformers onsite : we go round & round your agenda : one thousand small betrayals in the teeming heart of the interior : desperate sums in our throats : how did we get so stripped & scalded when all we wanted was to love ourselves : each other : this half-submerged raft of starmeat we sit on ::

we're speaking in code : things we think disguised as food : mineralogy or geo-tagging : adapt your pseudopodia to economic forces : wait-list your demons : translation becomes easier as we go along : stop expecting understanding & experience can happen : alongside every dog there is the shadow of its breath & bone : that shadow is made of words : thought is more than one man can eat in a lifetime : or one dog ::

when the structure cracks open & welcomes us : when the injury of days & the wind they bring : when the moisture of our words has saturated the walls : when making & unmaking have become the same action : when the light in our hands has the taste of honey : when the nails we pull up from the floorboards are songs : when eyes : when names grow : when names grow in the cracks : when night : we are there : we are with you : we rest our long hands upon your shoulders in blessing ::

the origami contrivances are burning : dead languages crisping & blackening between us, autumn leaves destroyed in a fish-gasp of protest : our crosswired failure : what i need & intend are signals from beyond the rim of your galaxy : the tune you want me to play is impossible for one of my species : so be it : no more false deaths : down payment for the big one : this departure is also the arrival ::

activate a mouth for every encounter : a validated task-flow complicated with need : eager walk to the square : secret walls to tell the nails & leaflets to : meet me at the war library : the attraction is bright & brave as a bell : your forested impulse works to keep up : sing the pain of will, of wonder ::

the nothingness that gleams in the night can lead to mistaken desires : you don't know what you're asking for : new darkening dust winters over while the distance shrinks : every day a bigger doll turns up on the doormat : it's a dance, like carbon tetrachloride : they push, you push, meat gets made : it's said there's a vehicle that runs on pure nausea : we should be so lucky ::

everyone speaks at once : a whistle goes off in the manufacturing sector : the masks slip & the tasters wait : a dozen flung birds bait us with silence : an egg, a temblor : nonstandard & weak : it's best we don't follow : we stick to the sockets & pray for solidity : naff ink snack in hand ::

this wind has a heart that stretches : portals & stairways enveloped in the skin of its breath : the need to dance is strong : carried in the membrane of wind : the soft structure of weather : there can be silence amid great sound : the droplet of void amid chaos & the shell game : pivot of my swirling eye, my dark matter, all limits & stuttering tongue ::

who wants to play with my rainy day : my pony beam : my otherness : sitting on a hill overlooking the village it's easy to say i don't know where i am : where i belong : do those questions even matter : i have a head that flies up & down depending on necessity but never side to side : i wait for it to launch or land : my otherness sticks with me no matter where my head goes : fine, there's the sunlit clearing : let's go there : never loan out a rainy day you can't stand to lose ::

umbilical wilderness intrudes : a lake of sapients in contact with elemental forces : battering-ram holdouts in the next town confer with your ambassadors : they reach for the sky : they feel lucky : the knowledge of calm seeps in, wicking upwards from their trouser cuffs : my favorite aspirant, take your weapon from my hand : take the grip in your long fingers : it is the way of this world ::

hear the tent music from the hillside : a little reptile milk catches in your throat : how the scene can turn dark while the day holds its arms spread : a blithe assassin, a quirt : that thick, tame pistol everted & gleaming : on the hillside they can't guess our business : there's laughter in the pit : someone calls for quiet : there is the song of bread & the song of sand : there is the chain whose fingers burrow into the past : there is your mouth, open ::

we beat into the dusk : a penny on your forehead : my tongue of wind : i cold, i part, i cannon you into the void : this touch is only for us : this journey of mutual enhancement : how many bodies are we : how many selves : how many worlds ::

drink this twilight before it fades : my mouth is moving in your slow black hair : intrigue flickers in wet shadow : the bird alone in the sky, neck stretched into the aura of its destination : my fingers close around your wrist : the ivy climbs scarlet on the wall : aggressive blood of the beat of moments : who are we ::

the thousand galaxies commune in our hearts : the unknowing tribe leaps in : your knifepoint & the nick in the breastbone both itch in their memory : you cup my prosthesis, nudge the railing : a comfortable weight settles on our eyelids : we pitch & roll : our salient features awry ::

expletive deleted : ablative armor intact : the will to survive is strong : near-miss on an intercept course out of the system : out of body expectation : the cool gray gaze of the nebula : the fantasist who is the lover of long fingers & deceptive masks : the pistol in the hand of the serious seeker of balance :

erase the formula written on the back of my hand : erase the irritating slumber : erase the p
        a
            t
t   e
                r

                        n ::

trypophobic ancestors render me addlepated :
trembling on my tether : my god, this space : vast
& empty & echoing with wind envy : multiplied by
itself, itself, itself : stars are mouths : *what do you see*
: i see the past : the mouths that form the language
that speaks me ::

fall asleep & a small sound escapes : do not move the lips : conversation takes place between conditions : animals talking, or else : a morse thing thinking blips : a dark stairway in flyblown light : fall asleep & be only another animal : no more stage : no more ship : slow blood & membrane ::

our inclement source material dictates the behavior of our fingers : too much willpower in the winter : we separate from our journeys as if they could be sold like package tours : a trip to end all trips : a rose in the teeth : what you wish for without knowing why ::

prowling pink for saxifrage : approximate figures in the distance : whose intensity will be used for the gauge, for the ceiling, for the capitol : wobbly eye focusing freely : understanding night wind : the finial's cast shadow falling over the dish : outside it's architecture again & our oblique elbows : i didn't want to say anything : i think it's about time to fake your own death & start over ::

interpretation of cloud patterns : nephelomancy, yeah : specific meteorologies of desire : the choice to orient oneself to a certain direction : follow a certain contour on the terrain : collision of doubt & dream : we look to the skies for tomorrow's maps : we move roughly & in slow-mo into each other's arms : wow hey what the hell are you doing here ::

destined to the bunker : sharp call of thick grass : the bigger, better barrow-wight : i can't count blessings, not quite yet : the little yellow flower on your forehead : taste of your sweat : dizzy with dust & insects, we lurch onto the trail : definitions we brought with us can never see us through to the end : where does this sorrow come from : the stuff that unites our worlds : where did we learn it : bird nest wedged between bits of painted iron : please face the sun for i cannot ::

MAKING & UNMAKING

training day dawns over my depleted town : the jungle gym shudders : nothing to see here : nothing to be : paddleboat summer ends without interest, dry heart : too many pamphleteers rearing up on hind legs : it's like that every time : the folding game abuts the counting game : the counting game has nothing to say : one desperate tinsnip away from total ruin : what's a bank heist between friends : that significant porridge always failing to boil ::

nobody can be one thing all the time : any word meant to name is born a lie : it works like the tides or perhaps an accretion disk : collection, motion, transformation : unwinnable, despite propaganda : the inexhaustible fuel of my error : one day i will thrust through the shell of my habit : the work of maintaining coherence : one day, when day ceases to mean ::

a fragment of certainty breaks off & lodges itself in the throat : it takes over the larynx : everything spoken becomes a stone or a length of cable : sometimes two certainties meld : those words are twice the mass of others : the loss of indeterminacy buries relationships in mounds of rubble : dead cities weep ingots of lead : civilization crushes itself over & over : love is change & we have loved so much : the doom of petrification lifted by our confusion ::

the trend of the ivy along these walls & borders
: hands like hair, fiber in pods, flexing to tear
the travertine : a bad investment : taste brilliant
crimson if the sun hits it right, rind carrying about-
face little letters, steam : if you, brick, crumble into
incoherence : lost syntax structure voice seclusion &
venting : if that happens : blame the ivy trend : the
fad for wrappings & strangulation : human dodder
hooking into makework mortar : let's get really
really woody : spit on these spores : take them in ::

mollusk mentation in my momentary lapse : it's not what you expected : in a sore place where the triumph of minimization takes hold : in a home collected from its environment : think big : think like a : does it matter : years ago when asked if my lover thought *like a man* i could not reply : the question made no sense : the process of my own cognition timed out : the task remains uncompleted : the answer lies on the ocean floor : the answer lies : lies : lies : lies : lies : lies : think big : think up : superlative ::

exhaustion of the warmth of motivation : like remembering cash in your pocket but not which pocket : the hands ache upon waking : the thousand books of childhood : if your deer stride out of their apportioned preserve : if your lights scatter : the real voice of the prairie will not stop you from moving : the bearded elk, the crayfish : impudent coneflower in your hand : it makes sense to wait : hear all these things, their choices : your habit of acting just to act : only the human does that : build something small & invisible why don't you ::

the air & the hand work in each other's territories : it doesn't have to make sense or convince adversaries : the hand asserts its being : the air mandates the behavior of the hand : smugness : a taut smile, the kind that says *i'd rather not smile but feel compelled to, coerced by externals* : the air of the external : the hand of the monitored : these relations stack themselves into a tower : in the end it's meaningless : still has value even if there's no bullet-point : me too ::

that bulky vocoder in your bin : can you predict its success : can you navigate the denial it promotes : a sense of astonishment, a road up a low mountain : the moan of acquiescence : these vague days tumbling into & out of awareness : time, in other words : you don't like it : your basic needs unmet by work : destructive noise & costly gadgets defibrillated ::

friends, there are some books you will not want to read : we dictate the phrases : not everyone can render honor to mighty nations : this trial of acceptance is beyond endurance : this sexual pivot : the machine of need that runs on yes, then no, then no that calls itself yes : a flutter of doom that wrecks the furniture : retry ::

our adaptive strategy takes it out of the park : developing one requires a team of entrepreneurs in dazzling costumes : for example : do you remember that day in the middle of winter : the sudden eruption of spontaneous mutations : it was right downtown : helicopters circled : i needed to sit down : i found a teapot & stuck my head in it : you put my hands between slices of bread & wrapped them with duct tape : the wind whistled : we were content ::

static, frost : patience : dark approaching the horizon, seemingly meeting at some point in the distance : acute attack of horse dreams : fourth morning i awake lost & whickering, mouth stuffed with hay : six apples orbit my head : tactile memory of daisies snapping underfoot : whose knees knock language into me : mystery of flocked helmet : my face in a shop window : dim flickering, single-point perspective again : taste of timothy ::

i'm cooling these crimes : imagining tight feathers reeling from overcast skies : a balm of simple pigeons applied to a landscape : a pink wall without mercy : battle cognate : attempted action in context : i'm waiting with a pendant of zinnia : attack of glandular wish : combat or not, crispy shell or not : a track that leads in a circle like the first five words : dripping with tesserae ::

sometimes a symbol stalks up behind : pokes a willow branch or a fern into some unexpected opening : at these times the world takes on new colors : a ripple effect like old glass : in one or the other parachute with sun diffuse & fortified : writing in silk on the bowl of the sky : awakening the long tides of interest : unprecedented involvement : the inspiration of irritation : the membrane that makes wonder & keeps it safe ::

ordinary merrymakers disturb the mahout who influences my progression : the point of this seems to be clear to everyone involved : unfortunate catalysts have to be considered : when in the past a certain hesitation emerged, we had to adapt : today a tinderbox still means a flame : it isn't that same shame that came from being alive : that one that meant something had happened for which you were blameless yet blocked & quarantined nonetheless : that meant your portion looked smaller than everyone else's, even if it was bigger : it's still bigger ::

my philosophers are all in love with one another
: disturbing, bizarre associations result from their
couplings : forays into polyamorous activity : this
approaches scientific inquiry : if four philosophers
suddenly orgasm, then freak downpour in cairo
: why has no one warned me : the wind takes my
hat away : i chase it like i chase conclusions : being,
matter, nothingness : ideal, will, order : someone
better kiss me right now ::

ADJUSTMENT DISORDER

the interior has debatable contours : from within i am in danger of becoming a cautionary tale : you ask for my coordinates : the transmission is unsuccessful : the number of walls surrounding me is variable : the sponsoring institution requires my updates on a regular basis : the transmission is unsuccessful : in the interior my purpose changes : i have failed to transform into an egg or a plaster saint : i have failed to become a girl, a drill, a tablet : what surrounds me now is unclear : the marketplace winks knowingly : gentlemen, we have our answer ::

too much talk : the distraction of the dim moment : hard-won silence : at times the deluge comes from beyond the body, impossible & drowning : the absence of release : we do our best : we attempt the sifting, the sorting of data : how are we to live in the eternal storm at sea : miles from any harbor : the world's brand humming with horror : the power to make our wounds sing in harmony ::

aspergillus : approach of night, allowances within a certain small pail : a doom reversed, say little sweeties in foil wrappers : inhale : say w o o d e n : say l a b o r a t o r y : say b a r i s t a : it all makes sense when you slow it down & look at it in your rearview : washtub meets mistake, makes matters worse : i have a handle on this : it's ergonomic : my seat reclines : aspergillus : approach of night : i n t e r r o g a t o r ::

just think of that song you heard : the belly the barrel-organ the timekeeper's call : this recollection changes whenever it is performed : allowances made for static & inflation : if we care about our memes, then what : a new regime : candy corn : lawyers : that song you once heard : all together we roll up into one pretty abominable ball : who wrote this joke anyway : that song : burnt fingers : elastoplast : mulberry ::

ears to the ground : compensatory laundering of motives : at what point does self-awareness become revisionist history : taking on too much responsibility or too little : the amazing thing is how one can stack each isotope-moment atop its brother : life is soup, not sandwich : our dirty fingers long for something linear to hold : licked like sugar from a stethoscope : nothing is what we think it is ::

exist in a state of unknowing : uncertain even of the edges of the body : skin overlaps vapor, nudges vegetation : become the air : become the pain of old injuries : impose limits : a dance makes mud of difference : tread the world into blend & blur : life surrounds & is surrounded by death : there is no opposite : there is no ideal : the cycle pauses, & then ::

nothing comes easily : some days are so dimly lit that orange & umber squeeze from the same tube : my appalling elephant raises its head : every moment brings another wink & flame : if mystery is the method, where is the meaning : another struggle against that overwrought metronome of classification ::

the flayed man & his heartthrob envelop both past & future : the graphic distance between selves : the spoken, in shark movement, sudden bunt to the left : now our medium teems with hemocytes : master, anneal us : we are but corn to those teeth : we are soon to be osseous caverns : our bodies working information from our world as if our lives depended on this : our bodies forced into matter, unprepared ::

the older i get the more things tend to blur into each other : the border between flesh & prosthesis pretty porous these days : the walk propelling my energy packet through the fields & particles of this place : when i die i will become a table : a map : a bowl of mashed potatoes : it's easy enough to change this body : hard to choose what to be next in that bardo of recycling where everyone looks at everything & claims an affinity : i will have so many hands & nothing to put in them ::

prepaid disaster, its lip on fire : emancipation is possible, though far away : teraflops of dream & dream & dream stored safely on pale humming servers : who pays for all this : who decides what space is & means & where it begins or ends : please ask me how i see myself : please ask, don't define : i love : that is the single unshakeable core of me : changes happen & my love becomes more possible : it coalesces, growing in its skin, a star from a nebula : my soul known by another name : i decide where i begin & end & what to carry the soul in ::

under the pardonable bridge of fear i learn to survive the worst of it : it's worth acquiring the skill to recognize motivations & the cues of liars : in late summer when the goldenrod takes on that dusty look : says *i am old & hungry & my roots shout feebly against my limitations* : in late summer when the trains pass : when each pair of eyes that meets mine on the street pierces whatever bag i've made to carry myself in that day : i wish to be pardonable too : dress for battle, my chest kept close to my chest ::

tornado school : how to believe in warnings again : how to take care as the howl gives way to silence : append the following items to your application : find the cellar door : there is no cellar door : the cellar is elsewhere, in another home : these belongings piled up over the past in a reverse archeology : we work to bury where we've been : gravity takes over : a body sinks into the earth : day turns into night : into another body : a body sinks into the heart : we sit on the floor beneath the doorframe : each occupying two rooms at once : hope for survival ::

seven of us started : how many finished : the timeline has a nebulous gap : hazy like the limbo in someone's hell : ask for our fortunes : we have nothing to say : our ears are full of mice : our tongues worry our auras : seven of us started : three immediately perished beneath the crush of the demand : space deceived us : we put our faith in baskets : in paper & crisis : the fates are mildly interested now : we who remain delegate our coffee : we paste our legends to the door : the link to some idea or other ::

the dead lands open & the night turns on its shadow : time is foreshortened : yesterday the winking eye of the power indicator communicated coded messages yet to be deciphered : human burdens have shifted : we heard it would happen : two riddles became ten : waterfowl ceased migration through our world : today our hands shake with the cold & the force of our desire : our genitals shift in their skins : who comes calling today : who invites comparison : who will be embraced by a deep loss & fingered quietly into oblivion ::

all these catacombs & flames : these maps of yesterday rolled up in the corner awaiting damage : urgent missives in the service economy : urgent replies : supply this demand : is everything a matter of clientele : i know nothing : i am as ignorant as a stone drill : on the corner of want & loss i drop my books in a repeating loop of slapstick : the pavement cracks & the taxis & limos pour into the chasm : their horns blare an opera of descent : the mass of my inappropriateness collapses in on itself : i have become the damage : i have become cause & effect : a life on the edges transformed into the singularity at the center of : the singularity at the center of : the singularity at the center of ::

codes : codices : the crabwise motions of clocks & what they convey : convenience of concept : context : i cringe in sudden terror : cradle my camouflage for comfort : cup my balls as though the tremors could shake them loose : the predictability of this action, something i grew into like a skin of ivy grows across a wall : *my* skin, damp with panic : calices erupt behind my ears : i cry out : tongue protrudes : air rasps my heart : my teeth are powder : my penis strains against my palm : terror : transformation : there is no name for this love nor the body it becomes : no name but my chosen : the walk i take today, tomorrow, round & round into yesterday : into before, into become : becoming : became ::

asphalt word : dream barrier : work sign reef coral placer charges : *beware* : *activities on the beach are monitored* : *do not approximate the larger rhythms of the tides* : *your life is not on the grand scale of this ocean* : the road stops well before the water's edge : you fragment, pounding wildly on the sand with fists frustrated by materials failure : the winking light is not your eye : forget everything you ever learned about ownership : that orange mesh fence that contains nothing but doubt ::

how to edit a life : revision of clusters of effort yields confusion & casualties : there is no worse error : i do it all the time : whose voice is mine, the qualifying pronoun, the name of a stranger : i turn my back only to fall on the mess & roll in it : a retriever with a week-dead gull : disguised as my own error, what more can i do : rank with outdated concepts & agendas unshakeable in work : my trembling hands reach for what i fear : i am the solution in suspension : chelate myself into a new man ::

what we wait for remains unreachable : not unreachable but undefined : we accomplish something, like a street or a piano : we plant a field full of a crop we enjoy : that is a wait we understand : waiting for the indefinable yields indefinable results : the wonder & the pain we feel when learning happens : the joy when failure ceases to fuel our insistence : is it enough to want & wait : to wonder at the little sketches we make of the world ::

how many ways to say that the body is light : in changing form i change the vibrating dream of personhood : the mystery more comforting than certainty : more real : i take my sex in hand : the weight of it, like the weight of my heart : the burst, the understanding of particle & wave : simultaneity only locked down by perception : i can travel for years & find you dreaming : touch your eyelids to wake you : in orgasm we fly apart, realign on new axes : the great flash of being, shared ::

i like the diamond that sprouts in the spaces between words : between assumptions made : it seems to be adaptable : in the blank earth sleeping diamonds resist names : in the flat plane of discourse they are a secret weapon : we grow into those spaces : wait for a sharp pulse of question : now : now : now ::

& these stars awake in your belly : & the anchor they form holds your body in the deep : & your limbs move slowly, more wave than matter : & each moment erases itself from your skin : & the question you were born with escapes : & your eyes close : & your voice leaps up, a little dog on your tongue : & your breath opens : & your hand : & your breath : & your hand ::

do not sing too loudly of the mastery of desire : the channeling of wanting into work : these wonders you place in your pockets for concealment : they are too important to hide : toss them into the air & walk toward where they land : compromise must be negotiated or it is not compromise : complicit in our own subjugation : our only recourse is harm reduction : we come to punctuate our hands with light ::

i am without wings : without puffballs or signposts or handbooks : i am without track lighting : geopolitics : bus routes : i am without a comforting aura of predictability : i am without inspirational footwear : or microphones : or hopeful alcohol : i am without small packets of candy : without crisply flapping pennants : without imitators : ninepins : bullets : driftwood : i am without that mosaic of infant lipstick : that generation-defining vocal turn : that thing—whatever it is—that drips butter onto the chin with clockwork regularity : i am without harmful irritants : a nest of needles : pumice : a ringed tail : forgive these deficits, though they doubtless threaten my manhood : there's much a man can do without ::

don't call us : we are many meters below the ground : if we open our mouths to reply, we will fill with sand : we are busy in our shepherd work : we herd vast families of model trains : we are amazed by the complexity of their lineage systems : it's all we can talk about : well, it's all we ever post in our status updates : so don't call us : we prefer not to fill up with sand : or moss : or tiny pebbles : wood chips : mulch : we are needed here : our trains run on time : our trains are healthy & have glossy pelts : they're breeding well : their young leap & frolic heartwarmingly : why not come down here & see for yourself ::

that grim drum beats in sleep : the pace quickens, thickens the blood : awake with a gasp, knowing there will be days between breaths if you do not : one door or twelve forces the feet to the floor : sand blows through the house, drifts in snake-backs across the boards : the tongue leans against the teeth for strength : this bad navy waits in the body for orders : who are we to stand with our hands around our great semaphores of work : we know nothing & can tell you all about it ::

the body between sleep & waking is a dim room in its own right : a quiet installation in a dusty gallery : a hum or a flash stirs the air : the location shifts : now a full dwelling painted with gloom opens out from parted lips : a hand loosely curled in a lock, dumb hasp left free : some words are visible in the corners of the body : addresses : names : questions scratched from transcripts of telephone conversations : yesterday, last week, a decade ago : they are maps for strangers to use : those little vague scratches on the backs of invitations : folded paper to rest the head on, again & again ::

they say it's best to take it in stages : short, declarative sentences : it's best : there's time for it all : they say certain sentences work best : it's best to use those : when time moves in its own interest, they say it's hard to fit into short, declarative sentences : it's best then to open the sentences : open the words out into small instants of occurrence : short, declarative : hardworking ::

MY INHERITANCE

i'm not interested in bombs or babies or smart ways to interpret other people's behavior : i'm a little kinescope or maybe a tortoise with long incongruous whiskers : at any rate i find my perspective to be unusual in most discussions : so trust me when i say that sometimes i want to bury myself in a pile of leaves until the wee families depart & the park gates close : sometimes i want to stand in a field of cows & sneeze for an hour : sometimes i want to drive down a deserted road to find the hidden ruin at the end & move in : these things feel reassuring : like bees, you know : how bees can find their homes even when their homes don't exist : or like a star, following in the rearview : pushing the motor in the heart to click & hum in hope ::

what's my name : i am a man : you don't know me : what's my name : say my name : my name is the sound of ice floes cracking & moving on the niagara river : it is the voice of the burnt lip : the door to the shed left open : i am a man : what is my name : my name is wild onion : it is nasturtium in the window box in late summer before twilight : what is my name : my teeth clamp the edge of the mattress : i roar : my name : my name in my hand : my name is fire just like yours ::

sorry doesn't hold a world in its fuzzy arms : the trust issues : the list of charges : there won't be a party : this is not a teleprompted debate : sorry doesn't do that : the month i spent in a tent at the bottom of a ravine : not an apology : a hostile takeover : the way a gift can be a demonstration of superiority : the way a hand extended in aid can be an indemnifying clause : the way i still look at you fiercely when your back is turned : stupid pretense at separation, who am i fooling : certainly not the galaxy pouring into my skull ::

the rack of cymbals in my body bashes together in accompaniment when i eat : circular jaw motion activates this percussive tribute : all i ever wanted was a quiet life : to pursue silence like a doe, arrow nocked on the string : what do i do now that i've brought down my quarry : i have shot silence with an arrow through the eye & now the noise is *in me* ::

someone waits to be let in : it's not my key that opens the door this time : it's a string of odd coincidences : supper's late & the one shoe in the corner has no meaning & that's it, there's nothing more to say : except the light keeps shining in the back : the moon without a mediator clanging against the rear wall : damn it all, my horse is loose again : it goes around telling everyone its name : what, if anything, can be done : two people who resemble each other orbit the same bookstore : we sell saddles & eye the shiny heels of boots : the door opens with a howl : in comes the audience with my horse ::

the dragon looks tired : on the facing page, an entire city is menaced by beet-greens & a plague of chamomile : if this happened to us, we'd have to leave : we'd be in tucson by now, or bangor : if this happened here we would commandeer a school bus & drive someplace where people lived thousands of years ago but is now devoid of human habitation : in the forests of the northwest there must still be cities populated only by moss & insects : i will go there : rest my hand flat on a rust-furred refrigerator & laugh in prayer ::

the forest will find you : teeth inexplicably erupting through the bark of aspen & oak : forty species of mold communicating across miles : make a wish : the forest will find you : quiet streams cluttered with leaf pulp : biomass breathing through your mouth : the forest will find you : mossy-armed elders bending to embrace you & your soft meat : the canopy of dream : that rich loamy love ::

life is about to change : i reach again for the flavor & image of fiddlehead ferns : in the hat as i walk they are slick jade curls : smell of green breath in moist air : the life within them excruciatingly strong : edible fossils moving backwards through time : to begin a life as a thing millions of years old : what can that mean : what can it mean in the black iron skillet ::

this dark projection can be a burden : outside at night the walls light up with files & questions : do i ask your intentions : is it time for that : the walls light up as faces crack into particles : why are we trying to consume time : why is the flurry of photons so noisy : is this ring the same one i started with : the walls are groaning with air & need : a hiccup could bring it all down : & the light is tumbling like fish over rapids to sweep us into a new mind : we are galaxies against the blue radiant signal ::

tendons tell stories : mystery tales of limbs that fit suddenly into larger interests : a path broader than before : in some cases the length of the foot increases almost as if it were helping to speed the journey : the day also stretches into one 365-part day & this is all in the service of change : electrolytes indicate effort : i can't believe it's started : the doom of hips recedes : dumb glacier of unwanted buffering : & now the mouth fills with truer teeth : the hands contain tomorrow ::

erasing one file : that's not what we're doing here : erasure is not the right word : recognition is the analogous process : my today & my tomorrow recognize yesterday but do not attempt to obscure it : life in a derelict structure requires the structure to adapt : can i be held : can i shelter within this too-insulated form : the form has meaning only to the degree of its acceptance of my presence : my architecture rejects me : build something else ::

i scare the neighbors : circle in my biplane over the garage : fling heavy forks with vim into gardens : activate padded porch-swings as sites of resistance : the occupied zone is so quiet : the line of lights out of the city is desperate & hyphenated : i wish upon a broken window : signal my friends in the next county : bank slowly toward the north & ascend ::

i want nothing but my : i want nothing but the forest accelerating relentlessly toward the horizon : i want nothing but the wings i dropped in a ravine upon my mistaken puberty : i want nothing but : i want nothing but feet that proclaim me a captive of silver pines & radishes : i want no : no thing but : thing buttressed by idea, concept by name, head by stunning park-like landscape : i want nothing but the body with the land to support it & my supper in a bowl : both of which i made ::

during the day the signals shift & fade : impatience or uncertainty crop up on multiple frequencies : it's hard to stay tuned in : what are we listening for : what are we listening to : a dream like a golden ass or a golden bough or a bowl of golden grahams : antiquity holds role models for people like us : discourse likes to put them in a box fastened with woo-woo : i don't care what anyone says : i dislike bad behavior no matter what it wears : the far past is not my problem ::

my questions multiply as the migratory flocks close in : they erupt into the sky, join various groups in formation : it's not clear where they're headed : people love to track migrations : they feel their immobility validated by the movements of other creatures : my questions aren't all of a type : they join several different flocks : farmers complain about bird damage but nothing compares to the disruption caused by questions : some people are known to carry shotguns : just to scare them off, you understand ::

i am talking & the sand is listening : the grass edging itself into being once more is listening : the unprepared tree is almost listening : people on the bus are watching : people on the corner are watching through narrowed eyes : the woman with the stroller is watching my crotch & my chest & my eyes & her hand lurches spasmodically to touch her infant's head : i am standing in my body on the sidewalk & looking at the window : the reflection of my body is looking at me : what is different in me when i am seeing : when i am seen : when i am watched, clocked, monitored, yet not seen ::

separate your hazards : there is no map here : no app to work it out with : old stories about footprints & horseshoes don't make sense anymore : our lives are not to control : close to here there is a spit of land that sticks into the body of a small lake like the shadow on a sundial : there is a railway bridge along this spit : i can't cross this bridge : the gaps between the ties are too wide : i can't convince my brain that my feet will walk the ties, not the air & water : too much data involved in the process : one surface, one shape, one stimulus becomes indistinguishable from the others : there are many hazards everywhere i go : the only way through is the slow way : do not overtake ::

that sound is distracting me : like a forest but not as loud : the movement of blood through me : the ocean : schemes of evasion : crackling fire : popping corn : this weight passed from hand to hand : a baton of meaning in the relay between forms : can you hear that : broken pages, rats from the past, horses on the stairs again : everything's so loud : i know the names of things but their sounds combine in ways that can't be named : like a forest but louder : the ocean : distance : you know that sound ::

ORDINARY WEAR & TEAR

& what has it given me : a knot of oakwood polished into a shining fist : & what has it given me : discarded shopping bags stirred by wind & whipped into an ascending stream of plastic wraiths : & what has it given me : a nail in the wall with a hat hung on it : & what has it given me : hair, yes, hair : & what has it given me : a tiny motor ticking over in the belly, in the groin : & what has it given me : windows flung open onto the spring air, a rush of green scent & space : & what has it given me : this voice of bowl & door : & what has it given me : a path & a lichen-wrapped stone : & what has it given me : questions to answer, answers to form ::

distance & dishes accumulate rapidly : the time is now : my face pushes out uncertain stubble like trying on a new expression : is there a word for this : is there a wall for scrawling notes on : i'm still bleeding & i can't put my finger on it : the trail of a process invisible to outsiders : is it growing yet : is it growing now : in dark soil my root thickens : stubborn & strong ::

it's time, & the day is all boom & candy-stripe : we stop at the corner for marginalia : packets of data, bursts, little drawings in pods : snap to it : make a list of last wishes : eat a melon wedge, slowly, eyes shifty : ducks & drakes all down the hill until : count backwards from one hundred : try to remember if you left the car unlocked : in a flash, regain a clear memory of a long-lost hiding place : chocolate crumbled to gravel under a floorboard : dream of it ::

the marshals are circling again : memory states that my dossier's been stuffed by taurokathapsians : i'm the steer they want to rope : cowgirl fantasies without object, just wardrobe & action : i never was a good prospect : my four hooves planted too far apart : the tufted thing below my belly too apt to just let fly where i stand : big moon eyes : yes, those & my hard haunch unbranded : to have my say : to stay this way : this pasture speaks in good green words & i am happy listening ::

not exalted in the way you mean : spiritual, yes, but i prefer sodomy to piety : in turning the corner, i tend to look behind as well as ahead : this makes me seem forceful & tentative by turns : if you want to call this a byproduct of eloquence or marginality, that is acceptable : the knife does equal damage edge-up as edge-down : it makes no difference what you call it : this dicey proposition has ceased to invite engagement : all that's left is to sweep the steps & pour lead into the keyhole : this interview is over ::

the cities of the body are populated by question & answer : my form is that changeable beast : a work of time : the meat of me made of words : blood & cum made of words : the bright beam of piss made of words : the places i carry within me are zones of dispute : build me a body inarguable : a sleek torso like a book : it's silence i want to fuck me : silence or the mutter of pages turning ::

the man with dead words hanging from his body like sated ticks : the man whose door faces both west & east so we meet in the middle & pass through one another, out the other side : the man whose born body is an uninhabited region : the man who carries the teeth of fictional men in the flesh of his back : the man whose hands overflow with bunches of spinach : the man with wide gray eyes & a song draped across his shoulders : the leaning man in the doorway of clarity : waiting for recognition as the days climb the ladder : the man weeping with the pain of everyday erasure & negation : the casual cruelty of she : the man demanding to be ::

this wish i have for your blessing : imperative to speak of my deep admiration & no way to language it truly : no sense but scaly crouch to dance with those clawfoot people : *saurischian* : tell me how you like to say it : that species of love you can dig into like a hill of grain : sometimes it must be enough to wave my tail & sway : you can understand me : can you understand me ::

every morning there is the male milk-bath : the tenor happening steadily with a vigorous crackle like that before a storm : i become a reptile of meaning as i grow : at the end of the day my sex glows with the light of yes : saturated & rank, hidden within the cloacal lair : & when it emerges slick & hard you know what it means : what i am : what you are to me ::

sky-hopping, hoping for release : this near-autistic state of muffled perception : waiting : waiting : legally, i'm a man on the down-low : forced into the wrong line : the step-into-the-light of interview : the others flock to the television to sup at the shouting table : i bury myself between drops of ink & listen to the inner work : unable to determine who is on trial here ::

there is a certain nudity in this experience : deliberate exposure of the turbid self : the troubled life : preserved somehow, still, by attempts at silence : how many others like me are here in this gathering of the unchosen : unchoosing to be here : what bargain did they have to make with themselves to be able to sit here at all ::

the judge sits in a bucket & i think that's okay : the judge rides a dragon into the city from the suburbs : this is a county courtroom not a city one so that's fine then : the judge likes ice cream : no, not ice cream—soy ice cream : the judge snaps his fingers in time to a tune some passerby is humming : i watch the judge roll himself up in the state flag in the corner : he unrolls himself after a minute : he sits : the judge takes a small bird from the handkerchief pocket of his jacket : it is his own bird : it is green & blue : the judge stands up & does an imitation of a tree : the bird takes the judge's gavel in its beak & flies into the branches : my body fills with light i can't help it i've become the sky : here we go ::

who will share my pornography of meaning : the broken arrow lodged in my breast, in my side : who will lap up my sugary blood when the false front peels back & everyone sees the wrinkled new silence beneath : i wait, gleaming invitingly, legs spread wide, basket bulging : i shine in eleven dimensions : my skin is your skin, my mouth your mouth : who will consume the narrative body i make, who will devour my signifier : who will put their hands down my pants & stroke my subject position : the bleeding, humming thing i love in waves of hope & terror : who will read me now, today, tomorrow : who is there to spread my pages, break my spine, inhale : o god ::

if it isn't clear by now, then it's muddy : i still cannot explain : consent remains the only thing between interview & interrogation : the language i make is meant for me : is *meaning* for me : the way a cuttlefish calls out silently with its skin : like the spy said, *you get to recognize your own* : here we are & you wish me to talk & i must refuse : the language i make is not what you demand : i have nothing else to offer & what i am, well, it just won't do ::

now is a time for speaking secrets in secret ways : we say little in handfuls : we say much in air or stone : wind brings words as well, flowers blown from the tree : pelted against the wall of the building : secrets budding : desire : darkness : a demand to be seen, known : a demand to be taken, again & again, just as i am ::

ACKNOWLEDGEMENTS

The poems "the body between sleep & waking" and "& these stars awake in your belly" were first published in *The Buffalo News*.

The poems "hear the tent music from the hillside," "we beat into the dusk," and "the flayed man & his heartthrob" were first published in *Monsters & Dust*.

I am grateful to the editors of these publications for including my work.

The poem "i am without wings" was featured on the podcast "Make (No) Bones," curated by Toby Altman and Emily Barton Altman.

I am also grateful to the many people who contributed in various subtle and overt ways to the manifestation of this book. Thanks to Joe Pan, Martin Rock, Ian Bonner, Rupert Glimm, Toby Altman, Max Wolf Valerio, TC Tolbert, Trace Peterson, j/j hastain, Nicholas Alexander Hayes, David London, Joe Proulx, Susan Besemer, Tracey Besemer, Zoe Tuck, CAConrad, and Laura Goldstein.

JAY BESEMER is the author of many poetic artifacts including *Telephone* (Brooklyn Arts Press), *A New Territory Sought* (Moria), *Aster to Daylily* (Damask Press), and *Object with Man's Face* (Rain Taxi Ohm Editions). He is a contributor to the groundbreaking anthology *Troubling the Line: Trans and Genderqueer Poetry and Poetics*. His performances and video poems have been featured in various live arts festivals and series, including Meekling Press' TALKS Series; Chicago Calling Arts Festival; Red Rover Series {readings that play with reading}; Absinthe & Zygote; @Salon 2014 and Sunday Circus. Jay also contributes performance texts, poems, and critical essays to numerous publications including *Nerve Lantern: Axon of Performance Literature, Barzakh, The Collagist, PANK, Petra, Rain Taxi Review of Books, The VOLTA,* and the CCM organs *ENTROPY* and *ENCLAVE*. He is a contributing editor with *The Operating System*, the co-editor of a special digital Yoko Ono tribute issue of *Nerve Lantern,* and founder of the Intermittent Series in Chicago, where he lives with his partner and a very helpful cat.

More Literary Titles from the Brooklyn Arts Press Catalogue

All books are available at BrooklynArtsPress.com

Alejandro Ventura, *Puerto Rico*
Alex Green, *Emergency Anthems*
Anaïs Duplan, *Take This Stallion*
Anselm Berrigan & Jonathan Allen, *LOADING*
Bill Rasmovicz, *Idiopaths*
Broc Rossell, *Unpublished Poems*
Carol Guess, *Darling Endangered*
Chris O. Cook, *To Lose & to Pretend*
Christopher Hennessy, *Love-In-Idleness*
Daniel Borzutzky, *The Performance of Becoming Human*
Dominique Townsend, *The Weather & Our Tempers*
Erika Jo Brown, *I'm Your Huckleberry*
Jackie Clark, *Aphoria*
Jared Harel, *The Body Double*
Jay Besemer, *Telephone*
Joanna Penn Cooper, *The Itinerant Girl's Guide to Self-Hypnosis*
Joe Fletcher, *Already It Is Dusk*
Joe Pan, *Autobiomythography & Gallery*
John F. Buckley & Martin Ott, *Poets' Guide to America*
John F. Buckley & Martin Ott, *Yankee Broadcast Network*
Joseph P. Wood, *Broken Cage*
Julia Cohen, *Collateral Light*
Lauren Russell, *Dream-Clung, Gone*
Laurie Filipelli, *Elseplace*
Martin Rock, *Dear Mark*
Matt Runkle, *The Story of How All Animals Are Equal, & Other Tales*
Matt Shears, *10,000 Wallpapers*
Michelle Gil-Montero, *Attached Houses*
Noah Eli Gordon, *The Word Kingdom in the Word Kingdom*
Paige Taggart, *Or Replica*
Seth Landman, *Confidence*
Various, *Responsive Listening: Theater Training for Contemporary Spaces*, Eds. Camilla Eeg-Tverbakk & Karmenlara Ely
Wendy Xu, *Naturalism*

Made in the USA
Columbia, SC
17 February 2018